WHY DO WE DO IT?

Leading Viking Captain Rolf Rottgutt Reveals All...

Shipmates...

People often come up to me and say, "Hey, Captain Rottgutt, what gives with the raiding and terror? Why don't you stay home and farm like everybody else?"

So I tell them:

• Fighting's fun, and if you're killed you go to Valhalla.

• Raiding is a profitable way of spending the summer.

• You can do all the farming you want in spring and autumn.

• If you want to make a name for yourself in politics, start by being a successful raider.

• And the look of surprise on people's faces when they see us coming is worth all the gold in Gotland.

Then people usually say, "Why are they surprised? Don't they spend their time fighting off invaders? What makes you so different?"

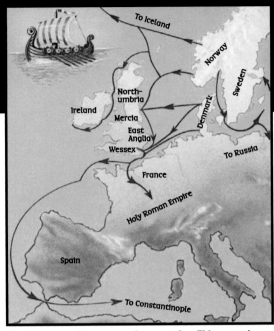

Here's a map for our readers, so they'll know where all the places we talk about actually are.

So I tell them...

• What makes us surprising is that we're so unexpected. People are used to being attacked by land, and usually get wind of it in advance. Us? We've got longships and can strike out of the blue. Before they've got time to say "Isn't that somebody coming to raid us? Put my porridge in the warm oven," we're all over them.

• And we go in and out of Europe's rivers like a dose of salts.

Then people ask how much I earn doing this, and I say:

• That's for me to know and you to find out. But I didn't get to live in a large house with several wives and lots of slaves just by being a farmer. Geddit?

Best wishes

Rolf Rottgutt

The Viking Invader

was written by
FERGUS FLEMING

and designed by
KAREN TOMLINS

Editor
PAUL DOWSWELL

Historical consultant
DR JOHN HAYWOOD

Illustrations by Guy Smith,
Rodney Matthews and Gerald Wood

SCANDS TO CLOUT
DEVOUT

Vics set for a kicking

789

Hang onto your hassocks! The Dark Ages are about to get a bit darker. Scandinavian traders are returning from expeditions in Northern Europe to report that unprotected monasteries and churches are stuffed with riches. "They're right on the coast, completely unguarded, and just ripe for hit-and-run raids!" Viking Sven Svansong told the *Invader*.

Church leaders are concerned. "It's an outrage!" said Bishop Cuthbert of Northumbria*. "Ever since the collapse of the Roman Empire we've been struggling to keep the light of civilization burning. And now these pagan Norsemen, or Vikings as they call themselves, will be coming along in their warships to ruin it all.

"They could even wipe Christianity off the map!"

Pockets

But leading Viking Captain Erik Frostbeard disagrees. "We have nothing against Christianity as such," he said. "It just happens that we're in the looting business, and the churches and monasteries are the only places that have any money.

"If there are any other pockets of wealth out there perhaps Bishop Cuthbert could let us know. We'd be very happy to display our even-handedness by looting and pillaging them too."

Captain Erik Frostbeard. A reasonable man in an unreasonable world.

ANYTHING TO DECLARE?

DANES' BRIT DEBUT ENDS IN BEHEADING

789

Offended Vikings have lodged an official complaint with Wessex port authorities, slamming the "extraordinary lack of respect" with which three Danish ships were greeted at Portland, on the south coast of England.

"Given that this was our first visit they treated us appallingly," fumed Captain Knut Hardefist. "I'm very much minded to give the place a miss in the future if this is how they welcome newcomers. They seem to be an aggressive, paranoid tribe of people."

Loot

The incident occurred when Captain Hardefist and two other officers docked unannounced at Portland, Wessex, for a spot of summer looting. The local sheriff, a man named Beaduheard, believed they were ordinary traders and immediately rushed down to help them fill in the customs forms.

"You can imagine how we felt," said Hardefist. "There we were minding our own business, when this bossy little man pops up and spouts on about unauthorized trading. 'You must go and see the king,'

Hardefist meets Beaduheard. One of these men will come out of this conversation very badly.

he says. Well we lopped his head off and then we did the same to his retinue. After that we left because we obviously weren't welcome."

Late

King Beorhtric of Wessex is standing by his late sheriff's decision: "This is the first recorded incident of a Viking attack in England and Beaduheard was acting with my full authority. It's no good just saying you're here to inspect the local economy – especially when you're waving axes at customs officials. **If they come here again they'll get exactly the same treatment.**"

WELL AND TRULY LOOTED!

LINDISFARNE IN SACKING SURPRISE

Aethelbert. Unfortunately, his lemon sponge cake was not a hit with his visitors.

793

Monks on the English island of Lindisfarne were paid a little visit yesterday. And it wasn't the men from the Cowl and Tonsure Board!

Ex-monk (now a slave) Aethelbert of Aecclescake told the whole story.

Kettle

"We saw these square sails on the horizon and thought 'That's a lot of pilgrims. Better get ready for them.' But hardly had we put the kettle on than the ships rammed onto the shore and all these Vikings jumped out."

Stuff

"We offered them cake and ale because they'd obviously come a long way. But they didn't seem to want any refreshment. In fact, one of them said – and I remember this very clearly – 'You can stuff your lemon sponge cake.' It puzzled me at the time.

"They were big rough men, and they had no respect for our 150-year-old monastery."

Twists

"They hacked their way into our buildings, stole our treasures, set fire to the place and took us all to be sold as slaves. Frankly, I'm amazed they didn't kill us all. Perhaps they liked our cooking after all."

SAINT
TOLD TO GET LOST

"Position hopeless," says missionary

Vikings say: "If we went Christian, we'd miss out on all the fun of a human sacrifice. Get real!"

830

Us Vikings don't want to become Christians. That's the message we gave to St. Anskar, when he visited the Swedish town of Birka.

"It seems you have no interest in our God at all," the French missionary told the *Invader*. "Vikings I spoke to told me you had quite enough gods of your own, and another one would only make life more complicated."

Horrible

Anskar seemed a little bewildered when he told us, "Everybody is completely pagan. You believe there are spirits everywhere, and conduct horrible rituals to satisfy them. I've heard you even make human sacrifices to ensure a good harvest. Of course, I pointed out that this was not acceptable conduct where I came from. But people just laughed and banged me on the head with their empty drinking horns."

Point

Anskar admitted that although from his point of view the situation is bleak, he has hopes for future progress. He's quite encouraged by the fact that in Birka we are:
• selling Chinese silk cloth
• wearing Persian jewels
• drinking out of German glasses
• using European coins.
"So you're not completely uncivilized" he told us. "In fact, you're quite enlightened. In other towns Vikings aren't punished if they kill a foreigner. But in Birka they get a good telling-off.

"I wouldn't be surprised if Sweden turned out to be a very progressive place in a thousand years or so," he concluded.

Here at the *Invader* we think Anskar is being a little too patronizing for the good of his health.

PORTENT FLASH

837

Massive whirlwinds and a giant comet in the east with a tail three ells long are predicted. Monasteries on the Rhine can expect a prolonged period of carnage.

Conditions will deteriorate rapidly along the Dutch coast, and people living on the island of Walcheren can expect to catch it particularly badly.

Outlook for the next few years: medium to coarse.

The portent forecast for noon today.

SPLASH!!!

DUBLIN BOY GETS DUNKED

840

Norwegian marauder Turgeis got an unpleasant wetting yesterday when Irishmen drowned him in Lough Owel – their local lake.

The vicious Viking got his come-uppance after a bout of prolonged paganism during which he declared himself "King of all the foreigners in Ireland", killed everyone who disagreed with him, and built a capital called Dublin.

Grate

"King" Turgeis isn't missed by most. However, Irish sources say they are grateful for the town, which has nice views over the Rivers Liffey and Poddle.

"It isn't much at the moment. But our defensive wall is in tip-top condition," said Irish resident Ruaidri Ua Conhobair.

As it stands, the new town boasts detached family accommodation with a house and garden for each citizen, a king's residence, a market, and an area for public gatherings. There is also a major port which serves all international destinations.

Turgeis heading for a watery grave. He leaves behind a first-rate capital city.

HOW PETRIFYING IS YOUR PROW?

This week we're looking for the scariest sight in the North Sea. All you have to do is send in a picture of your ship's prow. The most frightening one wins! In case of a tie, complete the following sentence using no more than 12 words. "If I had the Emperor of Byzantium in a Half-Nielsson I would demand…"
Carve your entry on a stone and send it to us by Friday morning!

This week's prize is a voucher for two platters of Battered Cod Pieces at any outlet of Fish O'Hoy, Isle of Skye, Scotland.

NOT WHOLLY ROMAN

843

EMPIRE GOES BELLY-UP

Good news for us Vikings! Less than 30 years after Charlemagne's death, the Holy Roman Empire has become the Holy Roman Bits 'n' Pieces.

At the Treaty of Verdun the big man's three grandsons split the Empire between them. According to the arrangement, Charles the Bald gets France, Louis the German gets Germany, and Lothar the Nothing-in-Particular gets an odd, lumpy bit in the middle called Lotharingia.

Helmets

Why is this good news for Vikings? Because we've found that three small kingdoms are far easier to attack than one large, powerful empire.

So it's "Helmets off" to Charles, Louis and Lothar, and a hearty "Good Riddance" to an empire run by an all-too-effective interfering busybody who won't let a man have a hard day's plunder for a hard day's pillaging.

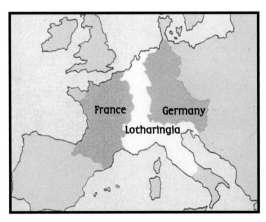

What's what in the Holy Roman Empire, that's what!

MOORS MOP UP

BOTTOM FALLS OUT OF SPANISH SACK

844

"I will never eat another orange as long as I live!" That's what Harald Steptoanssen is saying, having just come back from an all too pithy defeat at Seville.

Harald was part of the most adventurous Viking venture yet – to ransack southern Spain. The expedition started well, with an unconditional surrender at Lisbon, and an overwhelming pillage at Cadiz. But then, having sailed up the River Guadalquivir and given Seville a good going-over, they met a bunch of Moors.

Moor trouble

According to Harald, "We said, 'Who are you then?' and they said 'We're Muslims, but you can call us Moors like everyone else. We own Spain and we don't like your attitude. There's lots of us and we're going to thrash you.' So we said, 'Oh yeah? You and whose army?' That's where we made a mistake because they did, in fact, have a very large army."

Head count

The Emir of Cordoba, who controls most of Spain, spoke cheerily to an *Invader* reporter. "Yes, we gave them a very satisfactory seeing-to. We'd heard they were invincible supermen, you know. But we

destroyed 30 ships, killed 1,000 men and took another 400 prisoner. We made the survivors give us all their booty and sent them packing. Then we cut off the heads of 200 prisoners and sent them to the Emir of Tangier, in Morocco, to show him that the Vikings could be defeated after all."

Even moor trouble

Viking spokesmen are fuming at the defeat. Up-and-coming Captain Bjorn Ironside vowed revenge. "Me and my mate Halstein have got it all planned. We'll go

out there with 62 ships and burn all the mosques in Algeciras, sack a few places in Morocco, loot our way along southern France and then do Italy. If we've got time we'll swoop down on the eastern Mediterranean too. Then we'll sail back and do it all over again."

Bjorn even has his dates worked out. The time not to be a Moor is between 859 and 862.

> **The Invader says:**
> **See page 8 for more Arab antics**

Harald spreads the word among his fellow Vikings: "200 heads it was. Yes, it's quite disgusting..."

SLAP-HEAD DOES HIS TOP

Charles the Bald says: "No one will know, as long as I keep this fine gold crown on my head."

French Baldy Goes Ballistic

845

King Charles the Bald, grandson of Charlemagne, is hopping mad at the latest Viking outrage.

This Easter, Danish hero Ragnar Hairy-Breeks sailed up the River Seine and sacked Paris from top to bottom. King Charles had to give him 7,000 pounds of silver to go away without doing any more damage.

Thin

"It's quite atrocious," steamed the thinning royal. "And this isn't

the first time they've attacked us on a holy day. Only three years ago they cruised up the Loire and massacred everyone in Nantes on the Feast of St. John the Baptist."

Quick

"The worst thing about Nantes was that the Vikings didn't go away afterward. Usually they have a quick pillage, and then go back to their farms. But this time they camped out on an island for the whole winter, as if they meant to stay there forever.

"We can't have that at any cost, which was why I paid them all that money to get out of Paris. If they get the idea they can stay, then it's curtains for all of us!"

SLAVS SPELL SLAVES

The bartering begins... "A roll of red silk in exchange for 2,000 slaves. Are you trying to insult me?!"

850

'Will that be dirrhems or dinars, Sir?'

The men who put the Rus in Russia are sitting pretty. They've discovered a phenomenal new source of wealth – Arab silver!

The Vikings – or the Rus, as they're called down there – have sailed down the Russian rivers to the Black Sea and the Caspian and made the biggest trade breakthrough yet. The Arabs have huge silver mines, and they're minting coins called dirrhems and dinars which are used as far apart as Baghdad and Byzantium. What do they want for their coins? **Slaves**. And what do the Rus have boatloads of? **Slaves**, that's what!

Slav-tastic!

"It's wonderful!" said Helge the Horrible, member of a long-standing Rus dynasty. "When we settled here back in 800, we thought the place had nothing to offer but furs and wax. Then we went down the rivers and discovered these people with silver coins. And all they wanted for them was slaves! Well, look around you. The place is teeming with Slavs!"

The Slavs are mightily put out.

"We lived here long before the Rus came, and it's not right to take us over and sell us like this," said an angry resident of Novgorod, the Rus capital. "Life's a nightmare. Put one foot outside your front door and some hairy madman collars you for his next trading expedition. Life's not worth living. And I'll tell you something else. Know why slaves are called slaves? Because they're Slavs! The Rus couldn't even be bothered to invent a new word. All they did was take Slav and stick an "e" on the end!"

Scrape that barrel

Helge admitted that spelling irregularities occurred occasionally, but stressed that much of their merchandise was bought in, rather than simply pillaged. "Slav states are only too pleased to sell us the people they don't want. Criminals, debtors, convicts – that kind of thing. They make a profit, we make a profit, and the customer gets what he wants."

WHO'S ON THE MENU TONITE?

BIG BOIL-UP IN IRELAND

851

Irish citizens are in a pickle. They can't work out who owns their country. First it was them. Then it was the Norwegians. Now, it's the Danes.

"We're at sixes and sevens," admitted Feargal O'Conor. "Just when we had things settled nicely in Dublin, along came a whole load of Norwegians and drove us off. Then no sooner had the Norwegians arrived than the Danes came along and drove them off."

Boil

Astonished Irishmen say that when they came back to see what was happening, they found some Danes boiling up a cauldron on a pile of dead Norwegians.

"We don't know why they're so interested in Ireland," said O'Conor. "But we think it's probably to do with religion. We're the biggest bastion of Christianity this side of Rome. We've got some of the best monasteries in the world. And as you know, Vikings LOVE monasteries."

The Irish are more than a little upset at the way the Vikings are carrying on.

"We're Celts, right?" said O'Conor. "We've got a reputation for being bloodthirsty warriors – or we did have until we were converted to Christianity so you'd think they would have a little respect. Not at all. In they come and tear us to pieces. First one bunch, and then another. It's unfair."

Hey, hey, they're the monk-eys!

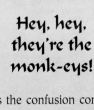

As the confusion continues, many Irish monks have decided to flee to a remote island in the north west called Iceland. "It's small, barren, and covered in snow," said one. "It's not very comfortable, but at least we'll be safe from the Vikings!"

They're cooking! Some Danes heading for Ireland.

CAPTAIN IN COFFIN BURNS WRONG TOWN

(Continued from cover)

"I asked if they were Vikings, because I'd heard there were some about, you see, and they said no they weren't and that they were only wearing their beards for a joke. So I let them in.

Sniggering

"They behaved very strangely. They all seemed to be trying not to laugh and I could have sworn I heard someone sniggering in the coffin.

"Anyway, they got to the graveyard and just as the service was starting, the coffin burst open and out jumped this bearded man with a sword. He ran the bishop through, shouting, 'Die, you Roman pig!'

"Well that really surprised us, because our town isn't Rome. It's called Luna. We explained the mistake to him and he got absolutely furious. He burned the place down, killed almost all the men and sold the women and children as slaves."

Gutted

"I'm absolutely gutted," Captain Ironside told the *Invader*. "I can only apologize to the boys. Obviously they were expecting some top-quality looting and all they got was this nowhere little town. To make amends I'm treating them to a first-rate brawl with all the trimmings."

DANES SPURN ARAB SMEAR

855

SPANISH SLAVER SAYS "IT STINKS"

Citizens of the Danish town of Hedeby were outraged to hear they'd been given the thumbs-down in a new travel book by Ibrahim ibn Ahmed al-Tartushi.

Tartushi, an Arab merchant from Spain who makes his living as a slave-dealer, wrote a damning report of Hedeby after his latest visit. According to him:
- the streets are filthy
- the stench is appalling
- the noise is atrocious
- rotting animal sacrifices hang on poles outside every house
- and the local singing is unbearable – "like the baying of dogs, only even more like a wild beast than that."

Locals are up in arms. "What nonsense!" said Horik Hammerhead, a prominent blacksmith. "This is a top-drawer, cosmopolitan trading town. We've had merchants from all over Europe and nobody's complained yet. If you ask me, we're a lot smarter than some of those so-called civilized nations.

"All you have to do is look at what's on offer in the market. Glass, iron, bronze, reindeer-horn knick-knacks, slaves – yes, they're all from Denmark! Apart from the slaves, that is. They come from all over the place – Ireland, Russia, wherever we go."

Jars

"What do the foreigners have to offer? Swords, millstones, and a few jars of oil and wine. Not much of a showing is it?"

Eric was even angrier at the suggestion that Hedeby has less-than-perfect town facilities.

"Outrageous!" he fumed. "Our streets are paved with best-quality wood. And our fortifications are second to none. It would take you a good day to walk through the Danevirke, our southern system of ditches and ramparts. If you wanted to look over the top of it you'd have to have three people standing on each others' shoulders!"

Tartushi isn't backing down. "The place is distasteful and utterly lacking in creature comforts," he said in a recent interview. "I strongly advise traders to come to Spain. We don't have as many slaves, but we do excellent lines in fine wines, flamenco dancing dolls, and letter-openers shaped like swords."

Hedeby. Citizens say, "We like a stench. It gives the place an easy-going feel."

SNAKE PIT DATE FOR HAIRY-BREEKS

Hairy-Breeks bites the dust – or rather a slithery, slimy thing bites Hairy-Breeks.

860

Ragnar Hairy-Breeks has been flung into a snake-pit by Ella, King of Northumbria. The Danish legend met his death with a smile and a cheery wink. "My sons will open your ribcage and let your lungs flap in the wind while you die a slow and horrible death," he foretold.

Rattled

Ella was unavailable for comment when our reporter rattled one of the 200 padlocks on his oak door guarded by ten squadrons of trained axemen inside a fort manned by some of the hardest soldiers in Northumbria.

"His majesty is treating the threat with utter indifference," a palace aid announced through the keyhole.

ELLA NOT A WELLA FELLA

Sons of snake-pit hero get nasty

867

King Ella of Northumbria got his come-uppance when the three sons of Ragnar Hairy-Breeks came looking for revenge.

Bleuughhh!

Ivar the Boneless, and his brothers Halfdan and Ubbi, did just what their dad said they would. They landed in England with a huge army called the Great Heathen Horde, marched right up to York, cut open Ella's ribcage and pulled out his lungs.

"We call it the blood-eagle," Ivar told our reporter. "It's one of our more impressive party-pieces. But you can relax. We only do it when we're really, really angry."

However, Ivar did admit that it helped their reputation. "If people think we're out-and-out savages it makes life that little bit easier. When they hear we're coming they just run away. There are all kinds of silly stories – that we drink out of enemy skulls, for example. Sheer exaggeration! But don't tell anyone I told you so."

Pressed

On being pressed, Ivar admitted that his Great Heathen Horde was another exaggeration: "It's not great and it's not a horde. Only a few thousand men at most. But we ARE heathens. That bit's true."

Whatever its size, the Great Heathen Horde has done pretty well. It's conquered the two Anglo-Saxon kingdoms of East Anglia and Northumbria and looks set to take over half of Mercia.*

Scrap

"New tactics," explained Ivar. "We're through with raiding. This time we're here to stay. But I have to say I'm very disappointed with these Anglo-Saxons. They spend so much time fighting each other that they've got no strength left for us.

"It's too easy. If you can't have a good scrap now and again, what's the point?"

"Heard any good sagas recently?" King Ella fails to break the ice with the sons of Hairy-Breeks.

OVER-DRESSED OVER-WASHED AND OVER HERE!

DANISH DANDIES
ANGER LOCAL LADS

Girls. Check out our *Invader* hunk of the month. It's dreamy Sven of Jelling!*

878

Conquered Anglo-Saxons are steaming at the latest Viking outrage. And for once it's got nothing to do with violence. They're complaining because the Danes are getting all the girls!

English lasses have been swept off their feet by the invaders' impeccable turn-out. According to sources, the foreign romeos are tops because:

• They always comb their hair
• They change their underwear regularly
• They have a bath every Saturday

"It's an absolute disgrace!" fumed Wulfric of Wallingford. "They come across all fierce and horrible. So we surrender. Then before you can say Jack Robenssen they're dressed to the nines and are taking out all our women. It's not fair. They're trying to have it both ways."

Reject

Olaf Smarmigitt, a highly successful invader, rejected claims that he and his men were taking unfair advantage. "We are a very well-dressed and well-groomed people," he said. "Of course we looked a bit rough when we first arrived. Even the best haircut suffers after a long sea journey. These Anglo-Saxons are jealous because we have superior personal hygiene and are tall, blond and dashing."

"They're a lovely lot!" agreed Ethel Berga from East Anglia. "It's a nice change to meet a bloke who doesn't look as if he's been pulled through a hedge backward or smell as if he's sat in a dungheap.

"The truth is that everyone's getting along fine with the Danes and a lot of them are marrying us English lasses and settling down here very happily."

HARALD WINS
HAIR VOW VICTORY

885

NORWAY GETS THE GO-AHEAD

Harald Finehair has become the first king of Norway – but it cost him a mighty big vow. He swore he wouldn't cut or comb his hair until he had united all Norway under one ruler.

It all began when Harald was jilted by a pretty princess who said she would have nothing to do with a man with no kingdom of his own. There and then, Harald made his haircut vow.

"It took him ten years," said court poet Thorbjorn Hornklofi. "And he looked a real mess at the end of it. By the time he defeated his enemies at the battle of Hafrsfjord, everyone was calling him Harald Mop-Head."

Mess

"It was a hard struggle," admitted Harald. "At times things got a bit hairy. But it was worth it. Before I came along the place was a mess – nothing but a bunch of squabbling kingdoms strung along a coastal trading route called the 'North Way.' Obviously things had to change. And I'm very glad it was me who did the changing."

Earl Rognvald of More, the man who snipped the royal dreadlocks, was enthusiastic about the state of affairs.

"Everything's hunky-dory," he announced. "We have a beautiful new country. Harald has married his princess. And the trade of upper Scandinavia is all ours. PLUS we get massive tribute from Lapland for the privilege of us not knocking their heads in.

"May I also take this opportunity to congratulate His Majesty on a magnificent thatch."

Finehair. Voted 'Thatch of the year' by Scandinavian barbers.

*Dreamy Sven's horned helmet is historically inaccurate, and worn only for effect. Vikings NEVER wear horned helmets. EVER.

KING ALF
SPLITS ENGLAND

ing Alf. A very good king, but (allegedly) no good at baking cakes.

886

"You're there – we're here," says Wessex man

Vikings are reeling after a stunning setback in England. King Alfred the Great of Wessex, who was defeated by the Great Heathen Horde eight years ago, has returned with a vengeance!

In a miraculous comeback Anglo-Saxon Alf scored a series of knockout victories which drove the invaders out of Wessex. He even forced his opposite number, Danish king Guthrum, and 30 of his top officers, to become Christians. Now he's finalized the business by making them sign a treaty saying who owns what.

Foot

"Basically, we were caught on the wrong foot," said Guthrum. "All our best men had settled down on the farmland they conquered, and there weren't enough of us left to raise an army to fight the enemy."

Under the new arrangement the Vikings have to stay in an area called the Danelaw, which runs up the east side of England. Everything else belongs to the Anglo-Saxon locals.

Cross

"Well, it could be worse," said Guthrum. "It's good farming country and I'm sure a lot of Anglo-Saxons will be crossing the border to live here. The advantages are endless. Here in the Danelaw – we invented the word "law" by the way – we've got a fantastic legal system, with local courts and a jury. They don't have anything like that in Wessex.

"What's more, we have the nearest thing to democracy this country will have for centuries. If you have 25 acres and a couple of cows you can come to one of our assemblies and join in with the decision-making.

"It's not quite what you might call a parliament or senate. I don't know what they call them in Wessex, but back home we just call them *Things*."

BYZANTIUM THROWS IN THE TOWEL

907

FREE BATHS FOR ALL

Russian Vikings were in a real lather yesterday as they celebrated a major victory over Byzantium.

Representatives of Viking King Oleg of Kiev sailed over the Black Sea to Constantinople, capital city of the Byzantine Empire. They walked around the city walls, and told the Emperor that unless he came up with a deal pretty quickly they'd sack the place.

They left with numerous trading privileges, open access to the city and the promise of as many free baths as they liked.

"Appearances are very important in this part of the world," explained Admiral Ingjald. "If you go into battle looking rumpled and grubby the enemy simply won't have anything to do with you."

Vikings setting up camp outside Constantinople.

STOP PRESS
GRAFFITI ANGER

Offended Byzantine citizens have lodged a complaint about a piece of Viking graffiti.

The offending runes, carved into a marble balustrade in their cathedral Hagia Sophia, read "Halfdan was here". Church authorities have launched an immediate investigation to find the culprit.

"Who are you calling smug?" says Rollo of Normandy. "I just happen to be an extremely clever Viking!"

CRAFTY KING IN SHOW OF NORMAN WISDOM

ROLLO TO RULE AT ROUEN

911

King Charles the Simple of France, great-great-grandson of Charlemagne, has pulled off a masterstroke. He's persuaded one bunch of Vikings to protect him from the others!

"I was getting fed up," said Charles. "Every year the Vikings would sail up the River Seine to attack Paris, and every year I had to pay them to go away. So I went up to th[e] Danish fellow, Rollo, an[d] said to him, 'Hey Roll[o] How'd you like to rule No[r]mandy? It's lovely. Got [a] fantastic capital at Roue[n] And it's really well place[d] on the mouth of the Riv[er] Seine. It's all yours. A[ll] you have to do in retur[n] is become a Christian an[d] promise to stop any V[i]kings coming up the river. [If] you're good, every ten yea[rs] or so I'll give you som[e] more land. How about it[?] Well, he almost bit my han[d] off, he was that eager."

Smorgasbord

Vikings are astonished by th[e] betrayal. "He's a two-timin[g] no-good son-of-a-smorga[s]bord!" fumed a Norwegia[n] raider. "What a turncoat!"

But Rollo isn't taking an[y] notice. He's got big amb[i]tions for Normandy. A[t] Rouen yesterday he u[n]veiled his plan to make th[e] Normans the most feare[d] people in Europe.

"We'll out-Vike the V[i]kings!" he boasted. "We['ll] invade Italy and Sicil[y] and best of all, we'll con[q]uer England in 1066[. And because I'm a man o[f] my word, we won't invad[e] France – not much, at an[y] rate – and we'll keep Pari[s] safe from invasion.

"Don't listen to wha[t] they're saying in Scandina[via]. I'm a sweetie really."

DANELAW DOWN THE DRAIN

954

BLOODAXE AXED

King Eric Bloodaxe of York is down in the dumps today. And not just because he's dead! Eric has just lost the last piece of Viking territory in England.

Eric, ex-king of Norway and now ex-king of York, did his best during a brief six-year reign to restore Viking control over England.

"He had an uphill struggle," confessed an anonymous source. "He had to fight off the Anglo-Saxons, who were gradually conquering the Danelaw. He had to defend himself against the Scots, who are a tough bunch at the best of times. On top of that he had to deal with King Olaf Sihtricsson of Dublin who decided he wanted a bit of the action too."

End

The end came when Eric was driven out of York by an army of Northumbrians and killed in an ambush. This left the way open for Anglo-Saxon King Eadred to march in and declare himself King of all England.

"Alas, poor Eric!" said Eadred. "He suffered the slings and arrows of outrageous fortune. Unlike me."

With Eric's tragic death his followers have thrown aside their swords and picked up their trowels. "We're through with all that Viking stuff," said a leading Yorkshireman. "No more raids and fear-some facial hair in the wee hours. From now on we're going to concentrate on allotment gardening."

But old habits die hard. Only last week three young men were found headless in a dark alleyway. Locals say they had scoffed at an ailing stand of runner beans.

Eric (far right), and his Viking pals pack their bags at York. Ambush ahoy!

POPPO DUNKS DANISH KING

HAND OF GOD AWES PAGAN BLUETOOTH

960

Following a sensational conversion, Harald Bluetooth, King of Denmark, has announced that all his subjects are to become Christian.

The breakthrough came when Bishop Poppo, a German missionary, told Harald he was going to prove that God was more powerful than Odin – by an act of faith!

"What's that when it's at home?" asked Harald.

"You just watch, matey!" said Poppo.

Red hot

The fearless bishop took up an iron glove, threw it in the fire until it was red-hot, then put his hand in it. Harald was so amazed he swore then and there to become a Christian, but he declined Poppo's invitation to shake on the deal. He was even more amazed when Poppo took off the glove and showed his hand was completely unburned!

"Luckily I had a barrel of water handy, just in case anything went wrong," said Poppo. "I told Harald to get in and then I gave him an all-over christening. Baptize-and-go, so to speak."

Harald is so impressed by Poppo's performance that he intends to book the bishop to convert the rest of his kingdom. Not only that, he predicts that all the Viking nations will be Christian by 1000.

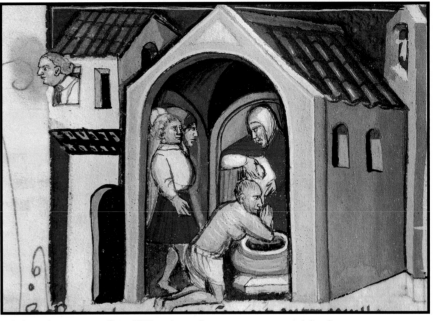

"Christenings are well cool!" Baptisms for commoners are rising in Poppo-ularity following King Harald's recent conversion.

BATHTIME MURDER HORROR!

Watch that soap! A Dane, yesterday.

1002

SUDS OF BLUD

King Aethelred the Unready of England has got fed up with having to bribe Vikings to stop attacking his country. In revenge he's ordered the death of every Dane in England.

The mass swoop came on St. Brice's Day, in November, when the Danes were taking their weekly bath.

Appalling

Almost every Dane has been killed. But a few survivors managed to escape and bring news to Sven Forkbeard, King of Denmark. Sven has vowed instant and appalling revenge, or at the very least the extraction of huge amounts of Danegeld.

Soap opera

"The English story that these people all 'slipped on the soap' does not stand up to close scrutiny," said a royal spokesman yesterday.

THAT'LL DO N-ICILY!

SETTLERS IN COLD RUSH

Iceland. A fine place for fur underwear, killer whales and turf. Not so good for camels, trees, fine wines and tomatoes.

980

Iceland is filling up – fast! One hundred and twenty years ago there wasn't a single Viking on it. Now it's got a population of 60,000 which is almost a quarter the size of Norway's!

When the place was first discovered, explorers reported that it was a paradise where every blade of grass dripped with butter. But when settlers started arriving, they found things were a little different.

Turf's up

"It's not a paradise at all," said one Icelander. "It's covered with volcanoes, ice caps, rocks and glaciers. Only one sixth of it is habitable. There are hardly any trees. The stone's useless for building. We have to make our houses out of driftwood and turf. Everything's in short supply. In fact, we're so poor that some people use bits of cloth instead of money. And let's get one thing straight – the grass does NOT drip with butter!"

So why's it so popular?

"Well," for a start we don't mind a bit of dis-comfort. Then there are all those kings back home bossing us around, and taxing us. It's nice to get away from that.

"The most important thing is that out here we're free! We're not a colony. We don't have to do what anybody else says. We're an independent state with our own government, our own laws, our own customs, and NO KING!"

Chips

"True, some of the laws are a bit odd. For example, you can't write a love poem to a girl in case you cast a spell over her.* That's a really serious crime. On the other hand, we have an excellent welfare system. If your sheep die or your farm burns down, everybody chips in to help out.

"All in all we're a progressive go-places kind of island. And we're so far from anywhere that nobody wants to raid us. So if you want to know why people come here, THAT'S WHY!"

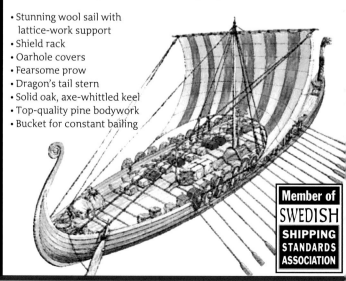
*Lovelorn readers may be interested to know that this is because Viking spells were composed in rhyme. A rhyming love poem therefore may have sounded very similar to a spell.

RED MAN IN "GREENLAND" SCAM

"I missed America," admits vexed Viking

986

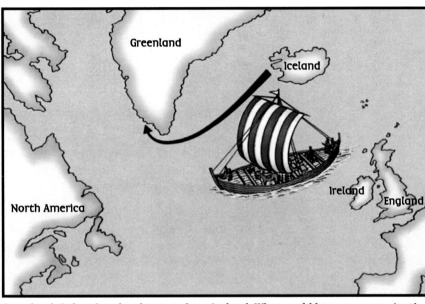

Greenland. Only a few days' voyage from Iceland. What could be more convenient! (Let's overlook the icebergs and bone-rattling winds.)

985

Erik the Red sailed from Iceland yesterday with 25 ships, ,000 colonists and a cheery wave. His destination? Greenland, the island that he discovered all on his own. But our exclusive scoop reveals that Erik's settlers are going to be very disappointed when they get there.

Shortly before he sailed, Erik confessed to an *Invader* reporter that he had been economical with the truth. "I called the place Greenland because I wanted people to think it was full of lush pastures. Those stories about Iceland dripping with butter gave me the idea. Of course it's nothing of the sort. It's a great big lump of land which is almost all rock and ice. But if I called it Glacierland nobody would want to live there, would they?"

Shady

Our investigative team

has shown that Erik has a shady past. He was thrown out of Norway for murder. In Iceland he committed several more murders before being banished for inciting blood feuds. It was during his three-year exile that he discovered Greenland.

The Viking Travel Association had angrily rejected bogus claims that Erik is part of their organization, and has issued the following statement: "Mr. Red is a seasoned outlaw, and people who travel with him do so at their own risk. Our reps have visited this so-called

'Greenland'. Although there are a few parts where it is possible to scrape a living, we advise Vikings not to be swayed by Mr. Red's promises of advantageous exchange rates and no landing tax. The usual VTA pledge of guaranteed pillage does not apply."

We all make the odd mistake now and again. But we don't make 'em like Bjarni Herjolfsson does.

The witless Viking got blown off course on the way to Greenland and found a new continent. But instead of landing, he turned away because it didn't look nasty enough.

"I was looking for Greenland," said Bjarni, "Not some place which may or may not be North America. What's the point in landing on a coast which has trees and grass when you know perfectly well the one you're looking for has snow and cliffs?"

Slam

Greenlanders are united in slamming Bjarni as an unadventurous dolt.

But Leif the Lucky, son of Erik the Red, has already bought Bjarni's boat and has declared his intenion of completing the job.

"I shall be sailing in five years' time, with a crew of thirty-five," he announced. "My objective is a place called Newfoundland, and if I don't find it, my name's Christopher Columbus."

GREENLAND UPDATE

Chill out! Greenland is booming. Despite an uneasy voyage, during which Erik the Red lost eleven of his ships, he has established two colonies and has announced his intention to create a new independent state.

"Even tourists are wel-

come," he said. "I give my personal guarantee that holidaymakers can expect sun-kissed beaches, nodding palm trees, little umbrellas in their cocktails and lots and lots of swimsuit activity!

"If the idle life palls, they can enjoy polar bear hunting, Eskimo spotting, seal

clubbing and a wide range of other invigorating activities."

Caution: The Invader *wishes to inform readers that resort inspectors have yet to approve the quality and/ or existence of Greenland's beaches, palm trees, cocktails, etc.*

BISH BITES DUST IN RANSOM BLUNDER

CASH FOR CLERIC CASE ENDS IN TEARS

The Aelfheah kidnap case comes to its unfortunate end. The culprits say, "Hey, these things happen!"

1011

"I was cleaning my sword and it went off."

Danish raiders have gone a step too far – even by our standards.

A fleet of Sven Forkbeard's warriors invaded England, and held Archbishop Aelfheah of Canterbury to ransom for the unheard-of sum of £46,000. But when the money was paid, the raiders got drunk and killed their hostage.

"We did everything they asked, following standard Danegeld procedure," said a church spokesman.

"We gave them a suitcase containing £46,000 in mixed denomination used coins. In return they gave us the Archbishop's head."

Left

"It was an accident," said Olaf Tufnutt. "And anyway, we left very soon after that. Isn't that the whole point of Danegeld? That we go away?"

The act has appalled many Vikings. In fact thirty-five Danish ships under Forkbeard's rival Thorkel the Tall have sworn to stay in England to protect the country from further atrocities.

Fork

"Doesn't matter to me what they do!" yelled an irritable Forkbeard to our correspondent. "When I'm writing out the next Danegeld bills I won't forget to put Thorkel's name on the list of people we need to intimidate. The little twerp."

SON OF UNREADY LOSES THRONE

DANEGELD PAY-OFF ENDS IN INVASION

1016

Danish King Canute has given up taking Danegeld. Instead he's invaded England and defeated Edmund Ironside, son of Aethelred the Unready. He now owns the whole country!

Behind

All I did was take precautionary action to make sure they didn't get behind in their payments," Canute told our reporter. "In fact I didn't want all of England. I only wanted what used to be the Danelaw, leaving Edmund with Wessex. But then he died and I was forced to take control. What else could I do?"

Fair

Anglo-Saxons are warned to expect 20 years of peace and fair rule, in which the country will be defended against further attacks and the rights of individuals will be respected.

Foreign

"Typical foreign do-gooder," grumbled local peasant Aedwig, of East Anglia. "He's breaking centuries of noble tradition. But I'll bet you a penny to a pinch of pig dung he makes a good job of it too."

"Oh we do like to be beside the seaside..."
King Canute's men get in the mood for an invasion.

THE INVADER SAYS

IT'S A DOWNRIGHT DISGRACE!

This is your captain speaking. Now hear this! The eleventh century is upon us, and it's the *Invader*'s sad duty to announce that the show is all but over. Once we were the top dogs! We were *numero uno* from the Black Sea to Greenland. Now we're history.

So what went wrong?

We started off all brave and warlike. But then we became soft. We took Danegeld instead of getting stuck in with our swords and axes. We stayed in the lands we conquered, giving everyone a chance to see that we dressed neatly and washed every day. (No good for the tough guy image, eh?)

It gets worse...

Then we married the local women and became Christian. Before you could say "Thor's Hammer" we were just a tall blond streak in the European gene pool.
Two centuries. That's all it took, from start to finish. Now, as far as most people are concerned, we're just a flash in the pan.

Settle down, settle down

But it's not all bad news. Things have settled down in Scandinavia – and the less warring and feuding there is at home, the less we feel the need to board our ships and go pillaging abroad. So let's look on the bright side:

- We built cracking ships
- We raided mercilessly
- We ransacked heartily
- We got ourselves a ferocious reputation
- We scared the tonsures off a continent of monks
- We defeated every nation and empire of note (well, parts of some of them)
- We discovered America
- We ate a lot of herrings
- And we drank vast amounts of beer

So let's look forward to a new era of equality and progressive taxation. And in the future, if there are any accusations of outrageous pillaging we can all say: "It wasn't us, boss. We've gone straight. It was the Normans!"

HIT AND MYTH WITH
Per's Petit-Point

Ladies! You know how it is. You're sitting by the fire, toiling over your tapestry, when you suddenly feel weary. You put down your yarn, sigh soulfully, and say: "Why should I constantly portray my husband in victorious poses? Why can't I make a wall-covering which really means something?"

SIGH NO MORE! PER'S PETIT-POINT IS AT HAND

Brighten up your home and keep icy winds at bay with YGGDRASIL, THE TREE OF LIFE. This exquisite piece of needlework depicts the Viking universe from top to bottom as created by YOURSELF! We supply the pattern. All you have to do is fill it in!

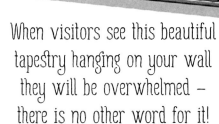

IT'S SO EASY

Just look at the exquisite detail we've packed into our tapestry. (Items in brackets indicate suggested yarn choices.)

 Yggdrasil – The Tree of Life itself. Connects all spheres of the universe. (Vivid brown, Light drab, Electric khaki.)

 Asgard – Where the gods live and play in magnificent halls surrounded by servants and followers. (Frenzy red, Beer cream, Mead yellow.)

 Jormungard – The terrifying serpent who lives in the ocean around Midgard. (Sea green, Snake green, Vomit green.)

 Midgard – We live here! (All shades inc. Burnt umber, Prussian blue, Carmine, Vermilion, Cerulian blue, etc. etc.)

 Bifrost – The rainbow which leads from Midgard to Asgard. (Poppy red, Fruity orange, Lemon yellow, Grassy green, Sky blue, Peacock indigo and Damson violet.)

 Niflheim – Horrible cold place you go to if you haven't gone to Asgard. It's freezing! (Ice blue, Snow white, Nose pink.) Also home to the dragon Nidhogg (Bile green.)

 Muspellheim – Horrible hot place you go to if you haven't gone to Niflheim. Sizzling! (Gas blue, Ember red, Feet black.)

When visitors see this beautiful tapestry hanging on your wall they will be overwhelmed – there is no other word for it!

Special Offer

FREE

with every order a poster of Hel, fearsome lady of the underworld. Top half: a dishy damsel – Phworrrr! Downstairs: a skeleton – Eeeeek!

Should YGGDRASIL, THE TREE OF LIFE disappoint, Per's Petit-Point can supply patterns of as many heroic poses as you desire. Simply darn your husband's features into the blank space.

Our Deluxe kit includes:

Pattern
Yarn
Needles
Full instructions
Wall for hanging
Nail for wall
Hammer for nail
Bandage for thumb

FINISHED DIMENSIONS

Height: Viking conqueror plus helmet.
Breadth: Saxon foe, minus head and legs.

Per's Petit-Point
Purl 1,
Threadneedle Street,
London

WRITE FIRST TIME!

WITH DANISH MASTER-CARVER NIBB HAMMERFIST

Welcome to the world of runes – that's Viking writing, foreign readers! If you've got something very simple to say then THIS PAGE IS FOR YOU!

"Writing? Who needs it?" A lot of people ask me that. And they've got a point. After all, we have an excellent oral tradition. None of our laws or stories are written down. We simply pass them down by word of mouth. But what if you want to put up a notice saying "Keep out", "Beware of the Dog", or "Kiss Me Quick"? Just try doing that using oral tradition!

So here goes! I'm going to teach you how to write runes. Follow my simple, step-by-step instructions and you'll be scribbling away in no time at all.

STEP 1. LEARN THE ALPHABET...

This is where we have a head start over other cultures. There are only 16 runes to remember. Think about it. Who needs d, g and p when t,

k and b will do instead? In fact, who need c, e, j and q either? As for v, w, x, y and z – **utterly useless**! What we've done is to throw out all the dross and add a second "a", a letter which stands for "th", and a capital "R". Easy!

STEP 1a). MAKE SURE YOU'RE USING THE RIGHT ALPHABET

In Denmark we use runes called Long-branch. Everywhere else in Scandinavia they use a scrappy thing called Short-twig. Don't mix 'em up. You'll look sloppy and people will laugh at you.

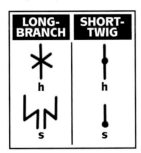

STEP 2. THINK OF SOMETHING TO SAY...

This bit's even easier. Make it short, sharp and stern. (You don't

want to be there all day, do you?) Try thinking of simple things like "Oric Was Here," and "This Is My Stone." Then go on to longer stuff – "I cut off Oric's head and buried him here," or "This stone marks the edge of my property and if you move one step past it, it's blood-eagle time for you."

STEP 3. SAY IT!

Get a piece of wood or stone, pick up a knife or chisel, and carve a vertical line. Congratulations! You've written the letter i. Add a few more straight lines and you've got all the letters in the alphabet. Why straight lines? You'll know as soon as you try to carve a curve! And another thing: horizontal lines are out because if you're working with wood a horizontal line can be mistaken for the grain. So there.

Right. You're literate. Get runing!

NEXT WEEK: I'll be telling you all about graffiti – PLUS how to carve your initials in a foe's forehead.

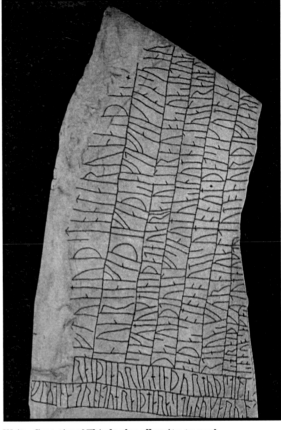

Write first time! This looks all write to me! No one would describe this as write-off! (Groan)

MEET THE AUTHOR

Nibb Hammerfist is the best-selling author of "Rune for your life: a history of headstones," and "How not to draw the Short-twig. Self-help for runesmen."

GO OUT IN STYLE WITH

GRIM'S GRAVES

THE DELUXE CROAK FOLK

Here's what you get with our no-holds-barred, elite, top-quality funeral package.

BOAT

Don't arrive unnoticed in Valhalla! Greet the gods in the manner to which you are accustomed with this top-notch raiding vessel. Comes with shields and extra-fearsome prow.

FOOD

In case you don't get to Valhalla; or if it doesn't exist; or if they don't have the dishes you like; or if you're just a big old hungry Viking. All items are by Hereafter Cuisine.

WEAPONS

There may be trouble ahead! Who knows what can happen when you're dead? It's as well to prepare for the worst. Anyway, if you do get to Valhalla you'll look pretty silly carrying nothing but a pen-knife – even if it does have a hoof-cleaning attachment.

SLAVE GIRL

Can't live with 'em, can't live without 'em! Our devoted servants are on hand to lay down their lives to serve you in Valhalla. They may not be willing, but they will. (Isn't it hard to find good staff these days?)

MOUND

Top quality soil, stones and grass, to hide the whole package from grave robbers.

LIVESTOCK

The spectral sounds of a happy homestead will follow you to eternity. Moo, Baa, Woof, Quack and Cluck. (Roar, Hiss and Trumpet not available – sorry, tropical readers.)

TOOLS

A busy corpse is a happy corpse. Everything you need for toil in the field, kitchen and workshop. Your slave will help you out if you can't face it.

ATTIRE

You've got to look good in the afterlife. They don't just throw their clothes on the floor and put them on again the next morning.

HOARD

Who says you can't take it with you? Pile it on. Gold, silver and ivory are supplied. Bring your own for added sparkle. But no coins, please, unless melted down into fancy bangles.

Sole Proprietor: Grim Goat-Shoe
Registered Office: Mound House, PO Box 77, Iceland.

Ooooh, yaargh, yowl. Arne at work, yesterday.

ONIONS

Dear Arne,
I was wounded in battle three months ago. Ever since then I've been staying with a friend who keeps giving me a revolting porridge made with onions. Besides tasting horrible, it gives me bad breath and appalling wind. What's going on?
Sigurd the Slayer, 11 Rottering Avenue, Kaupang.

Dear Sigurd,
Onion porridge is a standard test to see if warriors have been wounded in the stomach. If the wound smells of onions then it's a sure sign that you're mortally injured and are going to die very soon. In your case, however, it looks as if someone's got a grudge against you. Have you been sharing out the Danegeld unfairly? Or perhaps you've just outstayed your welcome? As the good book says:

"Even a friend becomes odious if he bides too long in the house of his host."

CHICKENS

Dear Arne,
I suspect my old friend Knut Knorr of stealing my chickens. Do you think I should take him to court? Or should I tactfully broach the subject over a horn of wine and ask if he has anything he would like to share with me?
Ragnar Tostig, Address Withheld By Request.

Dear Ragnar,
No, no, no, no, NO. You've got it completely wrong. Our society isn't about justice and understanding, it's about revenge. And this looks like the start of a first-rate blood feud to me. What you do now is to steal some of his chickens. He will then kill your cow. Your next move is to throttle his dog and poison his horse. He will then slaughter all your livestock and insult your daughter. When he does this, put on your fiercest helmet and burn his house down. He will respond by

NEXT WEEK: HOW

YOU WRITE, WE RIDICULE, IT'S THAT SIMPLE!

ARNE'S AGONY COLUMN

"BEST AGONY UNCLE OF THE DARK AGES!" THE ICELAND SAGAS

You can't put a foot wrong if you write to Arne. Whether you've got the plague, a nasty dose of something nasty, or simply a red face, Uncle Arne is at hand. Come to Arne with your problems. He'll always listen, even if nobody else will. This week Arne's spiced things up with some saucy snippets from the Havamal, a select guide to etiquette written by Odin himself.

killing your wife and pulling the bung out of your longship. That's when you chop him into little bits and feed him to his pigs. His sons will then come after you and hey presto! you've got a vendetta that'll keep both families happy for generations. Bear in mind that:

"A man who wishes to take another's life and goods must get up early. A wolf that lies in its lair never gets meat, nor a sleeping man victory."

EYES

Dear Arne,
I have noticed that Mrs. Next-Door keeps making eyes at me. What should I do?
A.P., 12 Lapp Lane, Stromso.

Dear A.P.,
You could do no better than read the following words:

"Be cautious but not over cautious; be most cautious with beer and another man's wife."

In your case I would suggest extreme caution as it so happens that I live at 13 Lapp Lane, Stromso and I am an exceptionally large and ferocious Viking. So is my wife. I shall be checking my beer when I get home, too.

HORSE

Dear Arne,
I'd been in Iceland a week when a local farmer challenged me to a duel. I was a bit surprised because I didn't think I'd done anything wrong. Still, not wanting to look soft, I went and got my weapon. Imagine my astonishment when he set this terrifying horse onto me. I barely escaped with my life. Is this how they usually carry on?
Harald the Hoofshaped-depression-in-forehead, 18 Elkbutter Mews, Reykjavik.

Dear Harald,
Ah me! You are a newcomer aren't you? As everyone knows – except you, it seems – Icelanders fight duels with horses. They get two stallions and let them knock each other silly. You come in when the fight is over. That's when you put on your sword and mail-shirt and accuse the other man of cheating. Then you have a merry old ding-dong and everyone feels better. Still, at least it shows you've got the right spirit. As Odin says:

"A coward thinks he will live for ever if he avoids his enemies."

BATS

Dear Sir,
Thanks for your answer to the above. But I have another problem. An Icelander asked me to play a game of football yesterday. Foolishly, I changed into my gear and trotted onto the field. Now I have a large wooden bat sticking out of my head. This is driving me to drink!
Harald etc. Ward 10, Stromso General Hospital.

Dear Harald
When will you learn? Football in Iceland doesn't mean snappy outfits and stop-when-the-whistle-blows. It means get as many men as possible, arm them with long sticks, and

attack the other side using the ball as an excuse. If you want something less violent, why not try all-in wrestling with cudgels? Anyway, keep off the booze because:

"Beer is not so good for men as it is said to be; the more a man drinks the less control he has of his thoughts."

THROTTLING

Dear Arne,
I'm a meek, well-mannered man. But I suspect someone of throttling my dog and poisoning my horse.

I've already stolen his cow. What else can I do?
Knut Knorr, Dunvikin, West Gotchar.

Dear Knut,
Please contact Ragnar Tostig (see above). He lives at 10 Golland Rd, West Gotchar. I'm sure you'll be able to resolve things. Remember:

"Do not break an alliance with a friend; your heart will grieve if you lose the friend in whom you can confide."

P.S. He told me your wife looks like the back end of a walrus.

Letter of the week

Dear Arne,
Horrors! I have a wart on my foot. I fear I may have picked it up at the baths. What remedies are available?
Nils the No-Good, Sea View Cottage, Lower Volga, Russia.

Dear Nils,
How unpleasant. Ugh! I would bet you contracted this revolting condition at your morning wash. How many times do you Rus have to be told? Yes, have a wash daily. No, don't all use the same water. It's downright unhygienic if several hundred people share the same footbath.
You could try making a sacrifice to the gods. Apart from that I haven't the first idea what you should do, except read this:

"A lame man can ride a horse; a man without hands can be a shepherd; a deaf man can kill; it is better to be blind than to be burned on a funeral pyre. A man with a wart* is of no use to anyone."

*In some versions this may read "A dead man..."

ACCEPTABLE IS SPITTING?

OPPORTUNITY AHOY

INVADER CAREERS SPECIAL

CONSTANTINOPLE: GLITTERING GOLDEN GATEWAY TO THE EAST

Vikings! Can you tell a Saracen from a sea-serpent? Do you know the difference between a barbarian and a bash on the head? Yes...?

Then Constantinople, glittering city of the east, wants YOU to join its elite brigade of Imperial stormtroopers: THE VARANGIAN GUARD.

Nasty surprise

Working under the direct supervision of the Emperor of Byzantium you will: wear a snazzy uniform, carry fearsome weapons, live in 5-star barracks, rid the realm of foreign devils, and protect His Majesty from nasty surprises.

And that's not all. You'll also have the opportunity to: travel the world (well, bits of it), meet people and kill them, keep the local population under control, and most important of all, get paid lots of money.

Bumpkins

And remember! The Emperor trusts the Varangian Guard more than his own army so he won't take just any old bumpkin. He wants the most feared of the most feared – and more than likely, that means YOU!

Top this

Not only will you get the chance to wave your swords and axes around in the traditional Viking manner, you'll also be able to lay your hand on a wonderful weapon that this Byzantine bunch have copied from the Greeks.

Ever wanted to try out a flame-thrower? Every night is New Year's Eve when you have GREEK FIRE – the top-secret napalm weapon used by the Byzantine armed forces.

Greek Fire burns underwater, on metal, on wood, on stone and on sand. In fact, there's nothing it won't burn on! And what's more, you just can't put it out!*

Prime location

And what of Constantinople itself? How will a hard-living, snow-and-ice-bound, axe-wielding chap like yourself find life in a well-to-do, balmy, opulent city?

*Archive fans: If you're reading this in the 21st century you'll be disappointed to hear that the formula for Greek Fire has been lost.

When you sail down for an interview with their recruitment sergeant, we strongly advise you to take up their offer of an introductory tour.

We think you won't be disappointed when you see what Constantinople has to offer. However, if you're really going to pine for those walruses, icicles, saunas and blood feuds, then it's best to find out before you sign your life away! Their tour takes in the following stupendous sights:

HAGIA SOPHIA

The world's most impressive church ever!

TOP SECURITY

Stupendous wallery, ditchery and bankery with unbelievable turretry, moatery and sea-barrierery. The ultimate in Keep-Outery.

HIPPODROME

The place to race your hippos. No, only kidding! Hippo comes from the Greek for horse, and this is the biggest and best race track ever. Seats 60,000!

(This week's Top Tip: Squiffy Theodora in the 3.15 Emperor Justinian Gold Cup)

Elite Viking forces of the Varangian Guard say, "The pay's great, and we're very popular with the ladies!"

TRIUMPHAL AVENUE

Three km (1.5 miles) of prime shopping and top-notch residences. THE place for parades where YOU will cut a dash after a successful bit of slaughter.

PORT

Teeming isn't the word! This place is busier than a sultan in a slipper shop. Gloat at all those goodies from India and the Far East! Silk, pepper, sandalwood, gems – you name it. (Not much of THAT back home, is there?)

POLO GROUND

Fancy a chukka? No probs. The perfect game for you tall, lanky types.

COURT REPORT

MURDER FINE WRANGLE

"Breaker" Legge, a resident of the Danelaw, is disputing a judgement passed by his local Thing.

Last Wednesday "Breaker" killed a man for calling him names. He was fined two pounds of silver in wergeld.

"Wergeld is the price you pay for a man's head," intoned Judge Birkchem. "Wer means man, as in werewolf, and geld means money as in Danegeld. Two pounds please, and don't let me see you in this court again."

"Breaker" is outraged. "This is out of order," he told a press conference.

"Breaker" in court.

"The victim was a no-good and worth only half that sum. If I lived in Anglo-Saxon territory I would be paying what he was worth to his master. Well, I've spoken to his master and he says he didn't even know he existed. I blame the Danelaw for its unreasonable insistence that a man is worth what his relatives say he's worth."

NO-VERDICT THEFT CASE GOES TO ORDEAL

The heat is on for the housewife who allegedly stole a bag of flour from a former friend. Due to lack of evidence the court has decided to give her a trial by ordeal.

Freya Isolde, who has always maintained she borrowed rather than stole the flour from next-door Brunhilde Ringsseikel, is jubilant. "This will show the world that I am innocent," she said.

Boil

The trial has two stages. First Freya will have to pick a stone out of a cauldron of boiling water. "If she drops it, she's guilty.

If she doesn't, she goes on to the next stage. Her hand will be bandaged, and if it starts to heal after a week, she's innocent.

Guilt

Legal experts are looking forward to the event. "If the evidence is inconclusive then trial by ordeal is a very accurate way of judging a person's guilt," said a Thing member. "And it's wholesome family entertainment too. My only regret is that the two women didn't choose trial by combat. That's just as effective as trial by ordeal and someone usually gets killed."

IN-LAW OUTLAWED

"And count yourself lucky I've not reduced you to slavery!"

With those words Judge Jarl Jelling ended the career of seasoned feudster Toke "The Terror" Torkspinn.

Toke's activities came to light after a series of spectacular murders and thefts transformed an everyday argument about the weather into a full-scale blood feud.

Horror

The 12 jurors listened in horrified silence as evidence showed that ex-berserker Tork had deliberately married into a family in order to escalate its feud.

"You are a menace to society," said Judge Jelling. "I hereby outlaw you for a period of three years. This means you are outside the law and anybody can kill you without fear of being punished. If I were you I'd get out of here quick."

Toke Torkspinn gets hounded out of town.

TRYGGI'S ROVING TOMES

The Only Mobile Library In The Dark Ages!

"Hey, good-lookin' Have you got my book in?"

THE AXE FILES

UNEARTH SOME OF THE STRANGEST SECRETS OF THE DARK AGES WITH OUR SHARP-AS-A-BLADE, JUST-FOR-FUN QUIZ!

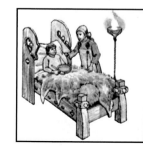

THE AXE FILES: IRRELEVANT BUT TRUE!

By our Trivia Correspondent – Arne Axe

Here's everything you always wanted to know about the world of the Vikings, but were too idle to ask! Pick out the most sensible answer, then check on page 25 to see if you're right.

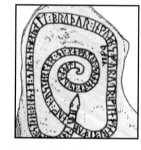

1. The word *Viking* means:
a) seasick
b) chewy walrus fat
c) plunderer
d) flaming red sideburns

2. The busiest rune writers were:
a) the Swedes
b) the Danes
c) the Norwegians
d) the Anglo-Saxons

3. Fashionable warriors wore:
a) flares
b) shades
c) snakeskin boots
d) velvet jackets

4. Imagine you were a Viking who supported animal rights. Would you:
a) stage protests
b) disrupt whaling expeditions
c) wear imitation fur coats
d) boycott major feasts

5. Harald Finehair, first King of Norway, had a great-great-grandfather whose surname was:
a) Fart
b) Snot
c) Poop
d) Kak

6. Vikings didn't have:
a) saunas
b) cold plunges
c) tooth decay
d) cavity-wall insulation

7. Ragnar Hairy-Breeks got his nickname because:
a) aged six, he won the Master Hirsute section of the Copenhagen Knobbly-Knee Tournament
b) he wore enormous, bristly knickerbockers
c) he was afraid he might meet a dragon
d) he never washed his clothes

8. Which grandson of Charlemagne was deposed for making a humiliating treaty with the Vikings in 887:
a) Charles the Bald
b) Charles the Fat
c) Charles the Simple
d) Chas the Wazzock

9. Viking streets were paved with:
a) planks
b) cobbles
c) the skulls of foes
d) concrete

10. To keep warm, the Vikings filled their walls with:
a) willow twigs
b) peat
c) wool
d) seaweed

11. The first piece of Viking poetry that rhymed was composed by Egil Skallagrimson:
a) to save his life
b) to woo shapely Miss Gerta next door
c) because he was at a loose end
d) to win a bet

12. York is:
a) a type of cheese
b) a Viking city with an important comb factory
c) the sound of someone being ill
d) an ingrowing toenail

13. King Athils of Sweden died of "immoderate joviality" while celebrating:
a) his divorce
b) the laundry finding his missing sock
c) the death of an enem
d) a really funny joke

14. Vikings felt ill in winter because:
a) they caught colds
b) they poisoned themselves
c) there was "something going around"
d) they drank too much blood soup

Arne and his axe. A marriage made in heaven.

5. The only promise a Viking was allowed to break was:
a) a peace treaty with a foreigner
b) that he'd do the washing up
c) that he'd be home before midnight
d) one made on a Friday

6. In Denmark, if you wanted to be a pirate you had to have:
a) a permit
b) a reputation
c) a big beard
d) a parrot and an eye patch

7. Vikings hunted elk on:
a) foot
b) skis
c) Wednesdays
d) horseback

8. Vikings made skates out of:
a) pieces of wood
b) horses' hooves
c) old swords
d) whale ribs

9. In 850 the Anglo-Saxons defeated a Viking fleet at:
a) Snak
b) Sandwich
c) Hamburger
d) Hottdhogg

20. The man who saved Paris from the Vikings in 885 was called:
a) Odo
b) Odon't
c) Hedid
d) Henever

CHECK YOUR ANSWERS ON THE RIGHT OF THIS PAGE...

MAIDENS ONLY

MARRIAGE
WHAT EVERY VIKING MAIDEN SHOULD KNOW

By the *Invader's* matrimony correspondent Great Aunt Freydis

An embroidery, yesterday. This is what you'll spend a great deal of time doing once you're wed.

Those of you who have not had the opportunity to travel will be unaware that Viking women have a great deal more independence and respect than women in other parts of the world. But like everywhere else, we still get married here. Before you lies a life of domestic bliss. So what CAN you expect? Read on, dear girls, and I will REVEAL ALL!

Finding Mr. Right

Your parents will usually choose your husband. You will probably marry for financial or political reasons, rather than love. (This is especially likely if you come from a wealthy and important family.)

Ker-ching

Before you marry, your husband-to-be gives your father a gift of goods and property in exchange for you. Then your father gives him goods and money for taking you off his hands. If this makes YOU feel like a bit of property yourself, don't worry – when you marry, all of these goods will actually belong to YOU!

Buuuurpp

Your marriage is celebrated with a huge feast. This sounds quite fun, but expect to see ghastly Uncle Harald from Uppsala, and dreary Aunt Asa from Trelleborg. The bad news is – if you're really rich the party could go on for a WHOLE MONTH.

The torture never stops

Unless you're rich enough to have slaves, your wifely duties will include: cooking, baking, brewing beer, making all the clothes your family needs, weaving blankets and tapestries, and (of course) looking after the children.

Oh no, there's more

Not only that, if hubby is a farmer then you'll have to milk the cows and feed the chickens. And you'll have to sort out all the household finances. AND you'll have to nurse any sick members of the family. AND you'll have to run the family business if hubby's off trading or raiding.

Grate escape

So what happens if twinkle-eyed Sven with the merry laugh and winning smile turns into a sour old goat who never changes his tunic. Simple. You announce you wish to be divorced in front of a group of witnesses and you're an older and wiser FREE WOMAN. Not only that, you get to keep the goods and property you brought to the marriage in the first place. NOT BAD EH? (Mind you, sour old Sven can divorce you just as easily, so go easy on the nagging!)

NEXT WEEK: FRESH WAYS WITH HERRING

THE AXE FILES
THE ANSWERS!

1. c) Viking means "plunderer". **2.** a) The Swedes by a long way. Rune-stone tally: Sweden 2,500, Denmark 180, Norway 45. **3.** a) They wore flares – and they probably wore gold medallions, too. **4.** c) Trick question! Vikings weren't animal rights sympathizers. But they did wear fake furs made out of cloth. **5.** a) His full name was Eystein Fart. **6.** c) Because they hadn't discovered sugar the Vikings had better teeth than most people today. **7.** c) His wife gave him a special pair of non-flammable breeches in case he had to fight a dragon. They were made from extra-thick fur boiled in pitch and rolled in sand. But, by the way, some Vikings did wear enormous, bristly knickerbockers. **8.** b) Charles the Fat. **9.** a) Streets were paved with wood. **10.** a) Willow twigs kept them snug. **11.** a) The poem was in praise of Eric Bloodaxe, who was about to have Egil executed. Eric was so impressed that he gave Egil a pardon. **12.** b) Apart from being an important city, York had a thriving comb industry. They made the combs out of antlers. **13.** c) He died celebrating the death of an enemy. **14.** b) Vikings suffered from carbon monoxide poisoning. When it was too cold to venture outside, their houses filled with smoke because they didn't have chimneys. **15.** a) A Viking was expected to keep his word at all times unless it was a peace treaty made abroad. **16.** a) In the eleventh century, the King of Denmark made a lot of money licensing would-be pirates. **17.** b) They hunted them on skis, using bows and arrows. **18.** b) They used horses' foot bones. **19.** b) Sandwich, of course. **20.** a) Count Odo kept the Vikings out of Paris in 885 and drove them out of France four years later.

Odin and Frigg

It's warrior Odin, the father of all other gods, with his two nosy ravens, who tell him what's going on in the world. His wife Frigg, the mother goddess, is by his side. She loves humans and can see into the future. One look at this sail tells your enemies they don't have a future!

Thor

The god of law, order and thunder who wields a mighty hammer. Thor rides on his chariot with two goats, Toothgnasher and Toothgrinder. He's friendly but dim, and there's nothing he likes better than an almighty scrap. He's the perfect role model, and an inspiration to your crew!

Loki

He's Odin's brother and god of trickery. Handsome and clever, he can change shape to become any animal he chooses. But he's seriously evil too – and out to stir up all kinds of mischief. Just the fellow to put you in the mood for a good pillage.

Freya

The goddess of love and beauty will keep you company on those long, lonely voyages. But, as you know, she's also the goddess of death. What more could an axe-wielding, blood-lusting looter ask for...

Fenrir

Offspring of Loki and Angrboda (a giantess), Fenrir is a wolf who's chained to a rock. When he breaks free he'll bring about Ragnarok – the end of the world*. Gives your foes a clear message – it's certainly the end of the world for them!

Ymir

Strictly speaking, Ymir is a frost giant, rather than a god. As we all know, Odin killed him and made the world out of chunks of his body. Ymir is guaranteed to make your enemy's blood turn to ice in an instant.

*Myth fans! Ragnarok will be marked by very cold weather, the Earth sinking into the sea and all life vanishing. Only two humans will survive. (Just hope it isn't you and that ghastly bloke from Småland you met last spring when you were pillaging Northumbria.)

TOOT-DE-ROOT!

INVADER CULTURE SPECIAL

Who says we're only interested in looting and pillaging? Anyone who knows anything about us Vikings will know by now that we're quite a cultured bunch. And guess what – we even play musical instruments!

Flowers

Here at the *Invader* we're trying to nurture this flowering of musicality by GIVING AWAY 200 PANPIPES. These musical marvels come with the following features:
• Holes to blow in.
• Sturdy stash-it-anywhere wooden construction, which ensures long life – even on the most arduous voyages.
• A whole five notes AND THEY'RE ARRANGED IN ORDER! (That's a scale, to our more musical readers.)

Stomp, rattle and bite

Each set of pipes comes complete with the famous "Osberg Method" instruction booklet to show you how to play panpipes the Viking way. Follow our step-by-step guide and within a week you'll be playing some of the foot-stompingest, shield-bitingest sounds of the Dark Ages!

Evergreen

Picture the scene. You and your raiding expedition are out there at sea. It's sunset and all is as calm as a country mill pond. But the men are restless. Their thoughts are turning to dragons, sea monsters and that unpleasant little blood feud they started last Tuesday.

Your social success is assured when you soothe their fevered brows by serenading them with evergreen hits like – "The fjords are alive with the sound of panpipes" – "Supercalifragilisticexpialipanpipes" – "I left my panpipes in Trondheim Harbour" – "Heard it on the panpipes" – and more!

Piece of cake

Anyone can play these little wonders. If you're not whiffling and pheeping like a maestro in the space of seven days, **we'll eat your panpipes AND our hats**.

So, write to the *Invader* at once, to claim your free set of panpipes NOW!!!!

What's the catch? We only want to know your name and address, job, age, religion, shoe and hat size, axe partiality, beer choice, and preferred make of ship, so we can endlessly bombard you with enough junk-mail to sink an ocean-going longship, that's all!

Panpipes. What every Viking should never leave home without.

FASHION UP DATE

SIR AND MA'AM!

Raiding may be out of season. But that doesn't mean you can't DRESS TO KILL! Follow these tips, supplied by the Viking Valet Co, and look good whatever the occasion.

SIR

MA'AM

SIR. You will require the following outfit:

Skull cap – made of leather. Very handy for hiding bald patches. And if Sir pulls the top up a little it will look like a helmet and frighten passers-by.

Shirt and trousers – made of wool or linen. Trousers may be flared or straight, or bound at the calf with a band of cloth, depending on your immaculate fashion sense.

Wool tunic – goes on top of the shirt and trousers. Makes you neat and tidy.

Belt – to hold everything up. Can be removed speedily should Sir wish to tan the hide of any impudent young gentleman. Also a useful place to hang your purse or knife.

Wool cloak – covers a multitude of sins, e.g., a skinny chest or a huge beer gut. Do remember to keep it in place with a pin or it will cease to be a cloak, and will become an expensive piece of cloth lying on your vegetable patch.
 Do bear in mind that during winter Sir will probably feel the need for fur rather than wool.
 (Safety tip. For instant sword access, do ensure your cloak is only pinned over one shoulder.)

Shoes – handcrafted leather for Sir's venerable old feet. Goatskin is particularly popular.

MA'AM. We would suggest a nice ensemble in muted mud shades with fashionable summer tints.

Headscarf – Ma'am will have to wear one of them if she's married. We suggest it be white.

Dress – long is this season's style. But you may wear short sleeves should you wish to display your dainty forearms. Ma'am may like to take the dress in at the waist, if Ma'am has a dainty figure.

Tunic – two matching rectangles of cloth joined over your shoulders by straps. You will want to use brooches to attach the straps at the front, thereby at the same time both displaying your wealth and taste and ensuring that the tunic stays in place.

Chain – holds everything Ma'am may need for domestic emergencies: keys to lock up Sir's drinks cabinet; knife for when Sir gets peevish about the drinks cabinet; tweezers for that irritating hair on the chin; scissors for free herring coupons; comb so that you can make an unexpected rasping noise whenever you feel like it.

Shawl – a nice wool wrap-around. Once again, Ma'am will notice the need for a brooch.

Shoes – ladylike version of Sir's great big leather boots.

Both Sir and Ma'am may wish to choose a suitable expression to fit the above. For Sir we recommend the scrunched-up, desperate, got-to-get-raiding look. For Ma'am, the irritable, foot-tapping, when's-he-going-to-go scowl will be appropriate.

INVADER STYLE • INVADER STYLE

BAD HAIR DAYS?

BANISH 'EM WITH THE *INVADER!*

Braid with the best! Our headwear correspondent Snorri Bouffantssen shows you how...

We all know how important it is to have long hair and massive beards. It looks rugged, it impresses the ladies and above all it's what people expect of a Viking.

But what happens when your hair gets out of control? It hangs over your eyes, and when it's windy your beard blows in your face. So what can a poor Viking do? Try a few of these for size!

Hair lines

The Bjorn Borg headband looks stylish at home or on a raid (see pic on right, below), and is an essential hairwear accessory.

The Bjorn Borg (right) and Pull-The-Other-One.

Or how about "Pull-The-Other-One" braids. Top tip – if you're feeling dim, hang a bell on one of your braids. People can ring it to see if anyone's home (see pic on left).

Don't just stop at the top. The stuff that grows from your chinny-chin-chin offers hours of endless fun too! The "My-Chin-Looks-Like-A-Fancy-French-Loaf" is very fashionable. But don't go to sleep on the breadboard! (See main picture, right.)

As a stylish variation you could try "The Fork-beard" – named after our top client Sven Fork-beard. For that ultra-horrible pirate look try lighting the ends – have a bucket of water handy!

High fashion

Long hair can be as much of a drag for Viking women as it is for men. Three great styles are currently highly fashionable in the fjords.

There's the "Granny Knot", which is easily maintained. As your hair grows just tie more knots! Then there's "The Bor-gette". It's just like The Granny Knot but with a headband for those who can't tie knots.

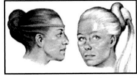

The "Borgette" (left), and "Granny Knot".

Finally there's "The Princess Royal" head-scarf, for married women only. Brighten up your headwear with a pretty design. Scarf patterns *en vogue* include: Fish-of-the-Sea and Axes-of-Asgard.

Warning. This man may look silly, but he can loot a monastery with the best of them.

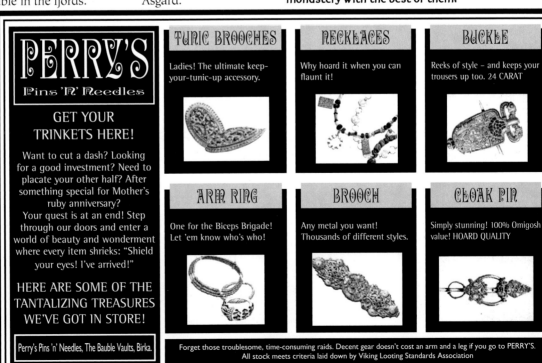

HALL ABOARD!
THE IDEAL LONGHOUSE

By our Homes and Gardens correspondent Leif Garretsson

The *Invader* is sponsoring the annual Ideal Longhouse exhibition at the world-famous Jarls Court in Oslo. The show is open for three months only. Demand for tickets is sure to be high, so make sure you take full advantage of our special offer, OPEN ONLY TO *INVADER* READERS (see main picture, right).

What?

So what's on at the exhibition? EVERYTHING, that's what! From tapestries to hat racks, beds to benches, WE'VE GOT IT. And, as they say in Trellesborg, if you've got it, flaunt it.

So what's the most unmissable exhibit? A full-scale reconstruction of the longhouse of your dreams!

Our longhouse comes complete with the following can't-live-with-out-them, no-expense-spared luxury features...

• Outdoor privy
Super private for those post-banquet moments when you need to be very alone. Don't forget to wrap up warm!

• Cattle shed
Situated in-house to keep you warm and comfortably smelly throughout the winter. Your lowing cattle will soothe you to sleep.

• Living quarters
For all the delights of communal living. No internal walls so you can keep an eye on everyone all the time. (But unfortunately this means they can keep an eye on YOU too...)

• No chimney
Cough, cough. Who needs fresh air? It lets in all sorts of diseases.

• Storehouse
Cold as an Eskimo's nose because it's outside. But it keeps the food fresh. (Separate salad compartment not included.)

• Floor
Packed earth. 100% soil. No cheap man-made-materials here! Covered with either reeds or straw.

• Central fire
Keeps you snug, does the cooking, melts the marshmallows, burns the fingers, etc. A most versatile household item.

Surely not

We're also sponsoring a SPOT THAT GOD competition.

Every day of the exhibition a member of our staff will be roaming the stalls dressed as Thor the Thunder God. See if you can spot him! If you think you've found him go up and say, "You are the bogus Thor and I claim my free prize!" Watch it though – we've heard that the real Thor's going to be there too, and he doesn't like being called bogus!

Winners will receive an immense stone hammer from Gods Kit and Klobber. It tenderizes steak to perfection!

A house is not a home without an iron cauldron of steaming oat and barley porridge bubbling away over the fire. What could be more welcoming?

Living quarters

DON'T MISS IT!

PROMOTIONAL FEATURE

IT'S...
EXHIBITION

FREE TICKETS WITH THE INVADER

MUST SEE!

Cattle shed

Our Ideal Longhouse has the very latest in pots and bowls, made from the finest quality wood-fired clay.

We also have a luxury selection of beautiful ivory drinking horns, custom-carved to your specifications.

STANDS TO VISIT

TIP-TOP TAPESTRIES
Breathe new life into your longhouse with our tasteful wall-coverings. Also useful for room-dividing and keeping out icy winds. **Stand 23.**

SONNY'S STORAGE SOLUTIONS
Barrels, large wooden chests and boxes of all sorts. Ask our storage specialist for advice. "Keeping you in the business of keeping things is our business." **Stand 10.**

LEISURERAID INC
Games, games, games. Get a life this winter with our fantastic time-killers. How about a game of fox-and-geese – played like chess but more Vikingly? Or how about chess itself – you'll love our walrus ivory chessmen. **Stand 15.**

LAMP-U-LIKE
However dank and dark your home is, we can make it lighter! Candles and oil lamps are what we do best. Cast a ruddy glow over proceedings with our amazing head-high metal lamp-holders. **Stand 4.**

CLOD 'N' SODS
Run out of wood? Living in Iceland? See us for all your turf-wall or roof requirements. **Stand 20.**

THATCHMASTER
We provide the ultimate in weather-proof roofing. On-the-spot estimates for reed or straw thatch. Wood tiles at ridiculous prices. **Stand 18.**

BEDS AND BENCHES
Scandinavian simplicity at its best. One horizontal surface serves two practical purposes. Sit on it – it's a bench! Lie on it – it's a bed! No tricky springs or catches. Clean Nordic lines. **Stand 53.**

MISTER PEG
Searching for somewhere to hang your clothes and weapons? Look no further! We stock a wide range of wall-mounted pegs to suit any occasion. **Stand 9.**

SNOMOBILTIY
Scoot hither and thither on our wooden skis, bone skates and sumptuous sledges. **Stand 13.**

LOOM-HO!
Busy, busy, busy, sew, sew, sew. Keep 'em at it. That's our motto at Loom-Ho! Try one of our trusty looms this winter. Your womenfolk will thank you for it. **Stand 22.**

FREE TICKETS
We are offering our readers FREE tickets. Just clip five coupons from your daily *Invader* and send them to the *Invader* in an envelope marked **Exhibition Marketing Scam**. We'll send you, by return post, one FREE ticket for every five coupons. **THIS OFFER IS LIMITED TO TWO FREE TICKETS PER HOUSEHOLD.**

IDEAL LONGHOUSE EXHIBITION

COUPON
DAY ONE (of five)

Please note: Your free ticket does not include a processing/postage fee of 2 filleted salmon – to be paid on entry to the exhibition.

1

INVADER CLASSIFIED

The Voice of The Viking

Want it? Lost it? Need it? Whatever it is you'll find it here. Just send your reply to the *Invader*, quoting the appropriate box number.

PLEASE NOTE: Ads are free. But please DO send them in on time. We go to press on Fridays and tend to be a little short-tempered by the end of the week. The *Invader* apologizes in advance for any impoliteness by any of its sub-editors, but it can accept no responsibility should tardy clients be hewn asunder and dispersed to the four corners of the room. We look forward to your continued custom. Thank you.

SITS VIK

LAW

LAWREADER sought by prominent Thing. YOU will memorize our laws and tell us what they are at yearly meetings. WE will mutter angrily and quarrel among ourselves. Excellent prospects. MI/5

SLASHING

ERIK the Throat Slasher requires PA for busy summer cruise. Duties include raiding, rune dictation and general mayhem. Must have steady hand and the ability to carve a straight line in wood, stone and flesh. NKVD/243

BAIT

RESPECTABLE Greenland firm, specializing in the capture of polar bears, seeks new blood to rejuvenate its fresh-bait department. Job satisfaction guaranteed. KGB/567

FROTHING

LOST your froth? Contact Ragnar Recruitment. We place more veteran berserkers than any other agency. SS/116

PILLAGE

RUSSIAN SLAVER needs persuasive Vikings to join his team of Opportunity Consultants. Full pillage benefits. OGPU/9876

HIGH FLYER

KING OF KIEV seeks new King of Bulgaria. Ability to let Vikings trade as they like is essential. No obstructors, demanders or pains in the backside, please. CIA/878

GROANING

VOLGA BOATMAN has vacancy for crew on river route to Byzantium. Must be able to groan in tune. FB/665

YOU'LL BE LUCKY

BORED LAPP, fed up trudging around after reindeer, would like to spend his time at home drinking beer. Do you have a job that fits this description? CID/932

LOOTING

LET'S LOOT AGAIN, LIKE WE DID LAST SUMMER! Knut the Knot-Very-Knice requires seasoned warriors to repeat last year's successful raid on France. Own beard, sword and shield please. PC/99

SALES VIK

Secondhand longship. Non-runner hence low price. Perfect for burials. SV/87

Complete set of Icelandic Sagas. Mint condition, still boxed. Would make excellent doorstop. SV/48

White flag. Never used. Will accept any reasonable offer. SV/54

Chinese silk. Fresh from Baghdad. Three rolls left. SV/67

Imitation fur coat, size 12. Ceremonial helmet. Child's toy axe. Three-piece bed/bench suite. Outlaw house clearance so must sell quickly. SV/91

Two places available on luxury cruise of Norwegian fjords. Unwanted prize win. SV/24

Ex-burial cart. Immaculate condition with all usual accessories – wheels, axles, sides, power steering, cruise control, chrome shafts, wood veneer, leather seats, etc. One previous owner. Goes like a rocket. First to see will buy. SV/75

CONTACTS

Miss Braid-head seeks Mr. Beard-face for cuddles and snuggly fireside fights. CB/32

Berserker, 32, wants to confront a lively lass. Must be used to foam. Barber's assistant preferred. CB/46

Looking for Mr. Write? Amateur rune carver, 25, awaits your call. CB/87

Nordic God, 48, tubby, patchy beard, warts, one leg, would like to meet blind Swedish stunner. CB/78

PHOTO CREDITS
© **Ashmolean Museum, Oxford** p11; © **Bridgeman Images** p6 De Agostini Picture Library, p13 t De Agostini Picture Library / A. Dagli Orti; © **Mary Evans Picture Library** p10 Carl Haag, p14 Carl Rasmussen; © **Pierpont Morgan Library/ Art Resource, New York** cover m, p2 r, p3 t, p9 bl, p16; © **Rapho** p12 tl Rapho/Belzeaux, Paris; © **Statens Historiska Museum, Stockholm** p5, p25; © **Tiofoto AB** p19 Tiofoto/Stockholm/Jan Reitz; © **Werner Forman Archive, London** cover b Statens Historiska Museum, Stockholm, p2 b Viking Ship Museum, Bygdoy, p4 National Museum, Copenhagen, p9 tr Universitetets Oldsaksamling, Oslo, p10 b Stofnun Arna Magnussonar a Islandi, Reykjavik, p13 b Statens Historiska Museum, Stockholm, p17 Statens Historiska Museum, Stockholm, p20 Stofnun Arna Magnussonar a Islandi, Reykjavik, p22 Biblioteca National, Madrid, Back cover National Museum, Copenhagen.

Every effort has been made to trace the copyright holders of material in this book. If any rights have been omitted, the publishers offer to rectify this in any subsequent editions following notification.